SALADS

SALADS

PERFECTLY PREPARED TO ENJOY EVERY DAY

This edition published in 2012
LOVE FOOD is an imprint of Parragon Books Ltd

Parragon
Queen Street House
4 Queen Street
Bath BA1 1HE, UK

www.parragon.com

ISBN: 978-1-4454-6756-6

Printed in China

Concept: Patrik Jaros & Günter Beer
Recipes and food styling: Patrik Jaros www.foodlook.com
Text: Günter Beer, Gerhard von Richthofen, Patrik Jaros, Jörg Zipprick
Photography: Günter Beer www.beerfoto.com
Photographer's assistants: Sigurd Buchberger, Aranxa Alvarez
Cook's assistants: Magnus Thelen, Johannes von Bemberg
Designed by Estudio Merino www.estudiomerino.com
Produced by Buenavista Studio s.l. www.buenavistastudio.com
The visual index is a registered design of Buenavista Studio s.l. (European Trademark Office number 000252796-001)
Project management: trans texas publishing, Cologne
Typesetting: Nazire Ergün, Cologne

Notes for the Reader
This book uses both metric and imperial measurements. Follow the same units of measurement throughout; do not mix metric and imperial. All spoon measurements are level: teaspoons are assumed to be 5 ml, and tablespoons are assumed to be 15 ml. Unless otherwise stated, milk is assumed to be full fat, eggs and individual vegetables are medium, and pepper is freshly ground black pepper.

The times given are an approximate guide only. Preparation times differ according to the techniques used by different people and the cooking times may also vary from those given. Optional ingredients, variations or serving suggestions have not been included in the calculations.

Recipes using raw or very lightly cooked eggs should be avoided by infants, the elderly, pregnant women, convalescents and anyone suffering from an illness. Pregnant and breastfeeding women are advised to avoid eating peanuts and peanut products. Sufferers from nut allergies should be aware that some of the ready-made ingredients used in the recipes in this book may contain nuts. Always check the packaging before use.

Picture acknowledgements
All photos by Günter Beer, Barcelona

Contents

Introduction

Mixed salads not only look appetizing and taste mouth-wateringly good, they're also a vital part of a healthy and balanced diet. The many different ingredients that can go into a salad are bursting with vitamins, minerals and, above all, fibre. Snacking on a small salad in between meals makes it easier for us to stick to the five-a-day servings of fruit and vegetables that nutritionists recommend.

Salads not only taste good in the summer, they also add variety to our diet throughout the year. Whatever vegetable happens to be in season, for example asparagus or cabbage, can be made into a delicious salad. Make sure that whenever possible you buy local, seasonal products: these have just been harvested and are transported only short distances so have maximum flavour. Lettuce has a high water content and becomes limp quickly, so it's best bought or picked in your garden on the day it's going to be eaten. Make sure the leaves look fresh and crisp. Lettuce should not be left to soak in water for too long, otherwise its many water-soluble vitamins will be washed out. It's also important not to keep lettuce in the refrigerator for longer than 3–4 days.

Avoid using bags of washed salad leaves from the supermarket because these will have lost a lot of nutrients and, in the worst case, may even be harbouring germs. Buy your salad ingredients fresh from your greengrocer or local farmers' market. If the ingredients are of a high quality, your salad can't go wrong.

Nowadays, salads are not only served as a small side dish to accompany a main course, they can also be a satisfying meal in their own right. They can be served warm with vegetables, fish, seafood, meat, pulses, rice, pasta or cheese, as well as cold.

Salads are therefore suitable as a small snack or lunch, or as part of a menu consisting of several courses. Fruit salads as a dessert are a wonderfully refreshing alternative to rich creamy concoctions and heavy baked puddings. You can also add a scoop of sorbet or ice cream, or some fruit purée or vanilla sauce.

In other words, there are endless ways to prepare salads! This book contains a selection of cold and warm salads from all over the world. From the traditional Waldorf Salad to the hearty Couscous Salad on Guacamole & Tomatoes to Beef Carpaccio with Parmesan Cheese & Lemon Juice, there is something to suit every taste.

Allow yourself to be inspired by our recipes and experiment with different combinations of ingredients. The look and flavour of a simple green salad can be enhanced with just a few additional ingredients, such as beansprouts, home-made croûtons, roasted nuts, seeds or kernels, edible petals, boiled eggs or baked egg garnishes, olives or anchovies – each time, a new and unique dish is created. Remember, too, that a simple green salad tastes and looks more interesting if you use several varieties of lettuce.

Dressings
A salad dressing should always complement and never overpower the flavours of the salad ingredients. For a salad containing lots of different, intensively flavoured ingredients, go for a light vinaigrette rather than a more powerful tasting dressing. When choosing oil for a salad, bear in mind that mild, more neutral tasting oils go better with salad ingredients with a stronger flavour. Strongly flavoured nut-based oils will complement the more bitter salad ingredients and add flavour to vegetable salads, such as a warm potato salad. Olive oil adds a Mediterranean touch to simple salads. Cold-pressed oils should be bought in small quantities and stored in dark, resealable glass bottles,

because they soon turn rancid if exposed to oxygen and sunlight.

Herbs

Fresh herbs give salads an additional flavour and an attractive appearance. Herbs also contain numerous vitamins and minerals. If you season with herbs, your salads will require less salt, so they will also have an additional health benefit. Salads and dressings should, for preference, be seasoned with fresh rather than dried herbs. Alongside classics such as dill, chives, parsley and cress, chervil, burnet, borage and lemon balm can also be used to flavour salads. There are endless ways to give your salads a new twist.

Utensils

To make a delicious salad, you don't necessarily have to buy additional equipment. All that's needed are good knives (possibly a curved chopping knife for herbs), a chopping board and different-sized salad bowls.
If you like green salad, it's worth investing in a good salad spinner. This spin-dries the washed lettuce leaves without squashing or damaging them and helps prevent sauces becoming too watery. When making salads with raw vegetables, a good quality, stainless steel four-sided vegetable grater is an essential piece of equipment. A small whisk will also make it easier to blend salad dressings.

For fruit salads, fruit scoops can be used to hollow out the flesh of melons or other fruit into attractive looking scoops. A citrus zester helps cut fine strips of citrus peel which can be added to fruit salads for an additional twist.

Using familiar ingredients you can create your all-time favourite salads – by introducing new, unusual ingredients, it will be possible to prepare an infinite number of salad variations. You can mix fruit, vegetables, nuts, seeds, grains, meat, and eggs in any number of combinations to produce interesting and delicious salads for every occasion – relaxed or formal, indoor or outdoor, winter or summer.

How to use this book

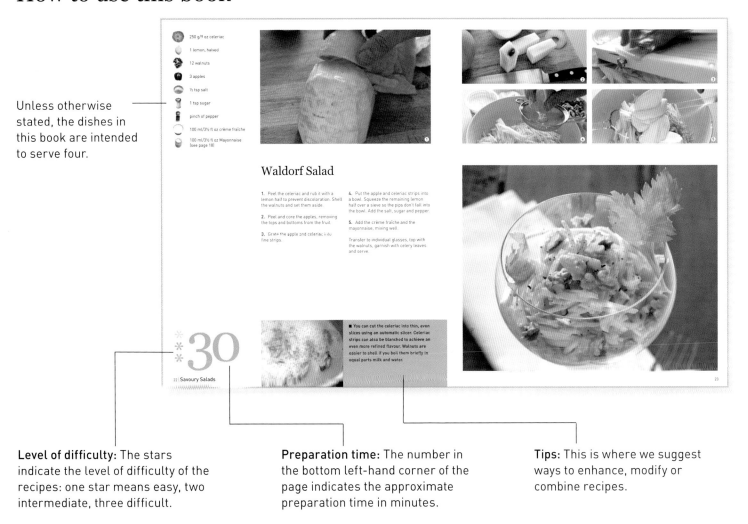

Unless otherwise stated, the dishes in this book are intended to serve four.

Level of difficulty: The stars indicate the level of difficulty of the recipes: one star means easy, two intermediate, three difficult.

Preparation time: The number in the bottom left-hand corner of the page indicates the approximate preparation time in minutes.

Tips: This is where we suggest ways to enhance, modify or combine recipes.

Lettuce & Herbs

Lettuce should be eaten as soon as possible after picking, otherwise it can wither and rot. Wrapped in a damp tea towel, it will keep for two to four days in the salad drawer of the refrigerator, depending on how fresh it is.

Fresh herbs can be stored in half a glass of cool water. Herbs will also keep for up to five days in a polythene bag in the salad drawer. Dried herbs do not like to be exposed to light or heat.

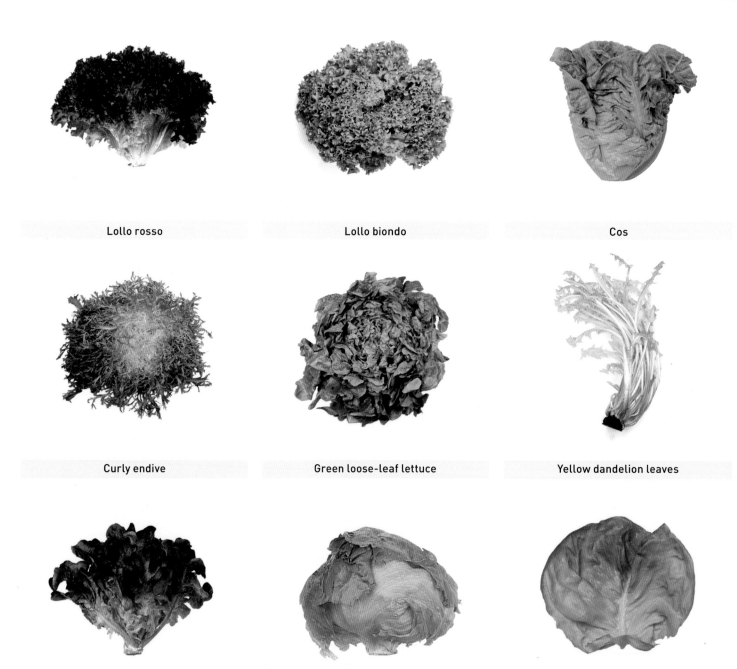

Lollo rosso

Lollo biondo

Cos

Curly endive

Green loose-leaf lettuce

Yellow dandelion leaves

Red loose-leaf lettuce

Webbs lettuce

Buttercrunch

Chicory

Radicchio

Red chicory

Rocket

Hijiki seaweed

Dulse seaweed

Beansprouts

Watercress

Purslane

Chives

New Zealand spinach

Parsley

9

Cos Lettuce

1. Cos lettuce should have a crisp heart, and the stalk should not be too dried out.

2. Cut off the stalk.

3. Cut out any brown spots on the ribs of the outer leaves.

4. Rinse the whole head under running water, then leave to drain well.

5. Cut the lettuce into pieces, wrap it in clingfilm and store it in the refrigerator.

6. The water will help keep the lettuce fresh for several days in the refrigerator.

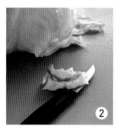
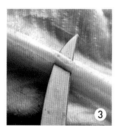
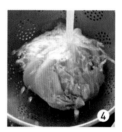

Green Batavia (loose-leaf) Lettuce

1. The lettuce should have a firm heart and the stalk should not be too dried out.

2. Cut off about 2 cm/¾ inch of the stalk together with any wilted tips.

3. Place the lettuce in a large colander and separate the leaves under running water to remove any dirt.

4. Rinse the leaves well under running water, removing any rotten pieces at the same time. Let the leaves drip dry or shake them dry. Place in a bowl, then cover with clingfilm and store in the refrigerator for later use.

Dicing Onions

1. Cut the peeled onion in half lengthways.

2. Using a sharp knife, slice the onion halves lengthways. You should not cut completely through the slices at the stem, so that they hold together and the onion doesn't fall apart.

3. Make a horizontal cut at a right angle to the slices into the lower third of the onion half, cutting almost to the end.

4. Make another cut into the upper third of the onion half.

5. Now cut the onion half vertically to finely dice. By cutting through the onion half twice, as described above, fine dice will be created.

6. The stem end, which held the slices together, will be left over.

7. Cut as much onion as possible from the stem end to avoid excessive waste.

Preparing Spring Onions with Green Tops

1. Depending on the size of the onions, a bunch may consist of 3–5 onions.

2. Cut off the upper third of the green tops and discard.

3. Cut off the root base.

4. Cut off the remaining green part at the top, which will be used later.

5. Remove the outer onion skin.

6. Cut off any bad parts of the stem base.

7. Cut the green tops into fine slices and use them as a garnish for salads.

8. The white part is best used raw, as young onions are not that hot, but are very flavourful nonetheless.

   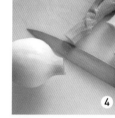

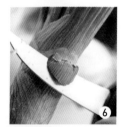

Preparing Carrots

1. Cut off both ends of the carrots with a sharp knife.

2. Peel the carrots lengthways, then prepare them for use in salads by cutting them into slices or batons, or by grating them coarsely.

Peeling & Deseeding Cucumbers

1. Wash the cucumber and peel it with a vegetable peeler.

2. Cut it in half lengthways and use a spoon to scoop out the seeds. Cut into thin slices for a mixed salad, or slice very finely and sprinkle with salt and herbs.

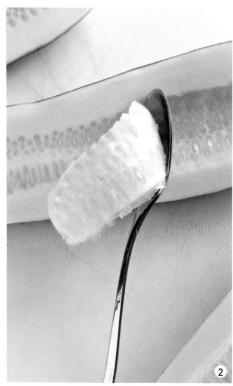

1 garlic clove

 1½ tsp English mustard

 pinch of white pepper

 1 tsp salt

 1 tbsp sugar

 4 tbsp white wine vinegar

 125 ml/4 fl oz extra virgin olive oil

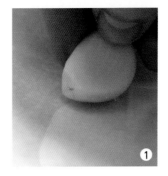

Classic Vinaigrette

1. Rub the inside of a bowl with the garlic clove. This is all it takes to lend the vinaigrette the necessary garlic flavour.

2. Add the mustard, pepper, salt and sugar to the bowl, then pour in the vinegar and stir until the salt and sugar have dissolved completely.

3. Pour in the oil. Stir with a whisk until a creamy consistency is achieved.

Makes about 175 ml/6 fl oz.

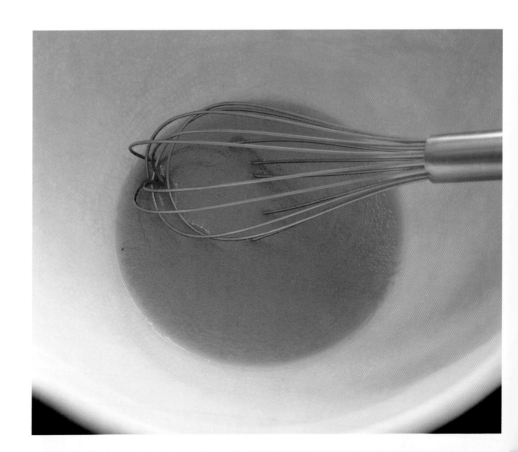

Herb Mustard Vinaigrette

Rinse ½ **bunch parsley, 1 bunch chives,
½ bunch basil** and **¼ bunch tarragon,**
removing any damaged pieces and finely
chop. Peel **2 shallots,** cut them in half
and finely chop. Mix all of the ingredients
with **140 ml/4½ fl oz classic vinaigrette**
and **1 tsp mustard.**

Makes about 250 ml/9 fl oz.

■ This herb mustard vinaigrette is a
good dressing for tomatoes, endive or
mixed salad.

Tomato Vinaigrette

Peel **2 tomatoes,** then deseed and finely
dice. Peel **1 shallot** and **½ garlic clove**
and finely chop. Rinse **½ bunch fresh
basil,** removing any damaged pieces
and chop into thin ribbons. Pour **4 tbsp
balsamic vinegar** into a bowl. Add **1 pinch
salt, 1 pinch pepper** and **1 tbsp sugar** to
the vinegar and stir with a whisk until the
sugar and salt have dissolved. Now stir in
125 ml/4 fl oz olive oil, a little at a time.
Add the tomatoes, garlic, shallot and basil
and mix well.

Makes about 250 ml/9 fl oz.

■ This vinaigrette tastes particularly good
on salads containing fish or mushrooms.

Soy Vinaigrette with Coriander

Rinse **½ bunch fresh coriander,** removing
any damaged pieces and finely chop. Peel
and finely grate a **2.5-cm/1-inch piece
fresh ginger.** Put the ginger, **4 tbsp brown
rice vinegar, 1 tbsp soy sauce, 1 tbsp
sesame seeds** and a **sprinkle of chilli
flakes** into a bowl. Pour in **1 tbsp sesame
oil** and **5 tbsp groundnut oil** and mix. Add
the coriander and stir.

Makes about 250 ml/9 fl oz.

■ Serve as a dressing for salads that
contain carrots, fennel or celery.

2 eggs

 4 tsp English mustard

 2 tsp salt

 pinch of white pepper

 150 ml/5 fl oz white wine vinegar

 pinch of freshly grated nutmeg

 600 ml/1 pint sunflower oil

 100 ml/3½ fl oz water

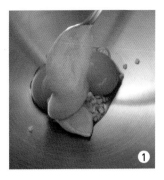

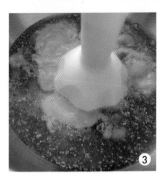

French Dressing

1. Separate the eggs, putting the yolks in a bowl. Put the egg whites in the refrigerator for later use. Add the mustard to the egg yolks.

2. Add the salt, pepper, vinegar and nutmeg to the egg yolks.

3. Mix with a hand-held blender, then gradually add the oil, then add the water and stir.

Makes 1 litre/1¾ pints.

■ This classic salad dressing goes with most leafy salads. It serves as a foundation for other dressings such as Thousand Island and Caesar dressings.

 15

Thousand Island Dressing

Caesar Dressing

Rinse ½ **green pepper** and ½ **red pepper**, cut them in half, deseed, peel and finely dice. Peel **2 shallots**, cut them in half and finely chop. Then mix everything with **500 ml/17 fl oz French dressing**. Add **2 tbsp tomato ketchup**, **1 tbsp sugar** and a **pinch cayenne pepper** and stir together. The diced peppers look like tiny islands in the sea – that's why it's called 'thousand island' dressing.

Makes about 850 ml/1½ pints.

■ As a simple variation, you can add a variety of pickles instead of peppers and shallots. Mix the pickles by chopping them in a food processor and add them to the dressing.

Grate **80 g/2¾ oz Parmesan cheese** and finely chop **1 tsp capers** (without the brine). Finely chop **5 anchovies** and crush them with the flat side of a knife. Fill a bowl with **250 ml/ 9 fl oz French dressing**. Add about **200 g/7 oz crème fraîche**, the capers, anchovies and Parmesan cheese and mix. Season to taste with **pepper**.

Makes about 500 ml/18 fl oz.

■ Mix in cos lettuce and finish with a sprinkle of crisp bacon strips and Parmesan shavings on top. This one is a salad classic.

6 eggs

 1 tsp English mustard

 1½ tsp salt

 850 ml/1½ pints sunflower oil

 juice of ½ lemon

 large pinch of cayenne pepper

Mayonnaise

Important: All the ingredients must be used at the same temperature; this means that the oil and eggs should either both come out of the refrigerator, or both be at room temperature.

1. Separate the eggs. Put the egg yolks in a bowl and put the egg whites in the refrigerator for later use.

2. Add the mustard and salt to the egg yolks and stir.

3. Add half of the oil, a little at a time, and beat vigorously with a whisk.

4. Add the lemon juice and cayenne pepper. Beat in the remaining oil.

Makes 1 litre/1¾ pints.

20

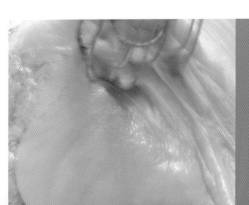

■ Lay a damp tea towel under the bowl so it doesn't slide while you stir in the oil. If the mayonnaise separates, you can rescue it by carefully beating the mayonnaise on the side of the bowl. The separated part will get mixed in a little at a time and the mayonnaise will bind again.

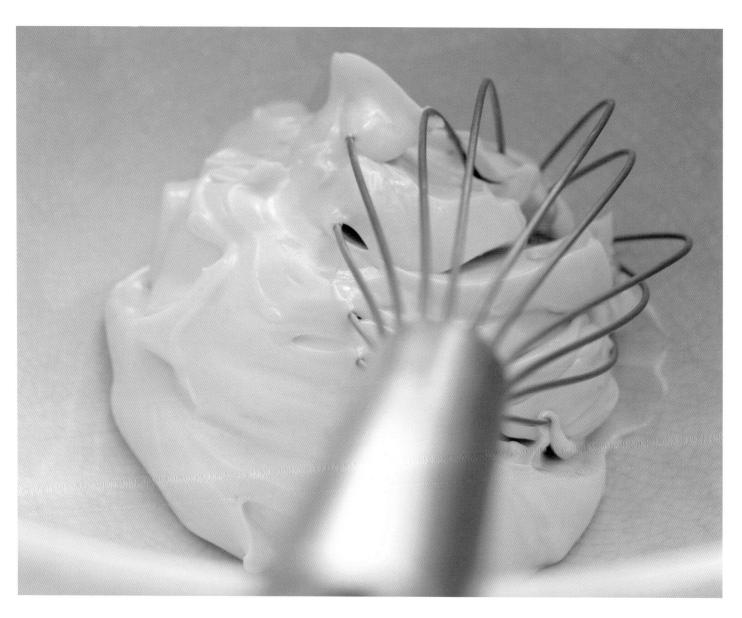

Tartare Sauce

Boil **2 eggs** for 10 minutes. Rinse the eggs under cold water and shell them. Peel **1 shallot**, cut in half and finely chop. Snip **1 bunch fresh chives** into small rings. Very finely grate the hard-boiled eggs. Mix the ingredients with **200 ml/ 7 fl oz mayonnaise**. Add **1 tsp English mustard**, the juice of ½ **lemon** and ½ **tbsp Worcestershire sauce**. Season to taste with **salt** and **pepper**.

To make the sauce a little lighter, add **1 tbsp soured cream**.

Makes about 400 g/14 oz.

■ **This is delicious with fish cakes or any fried fish.**

Remoulade

Peel **3 shallots**, cut them in half and finely chop. Cut **3 small gherkins** into thin slices, then into strips, then finely dice. Finely chop ½ **bunch fresh parsley** and ½ **bunch fresh chervil**. Finely chop **3 anchovies** and **1 tbsp capers**. Stir all the ingredients into **200 ml/7 fl oz mayonnaise**. Add **1 tsp English mustard** and ½ **tsp Worcestershire sauce**, then stir and add a **pinch of salt** and a **pinch of pepper**.

To make the sauce a little lighter, add **1 tbsp soured cream**.

Makes about 400 g/14 oz.

■ **Serve with roast beef salad.**

Rouille Sauce

Peel and slice **3 garlic cloves**. Peel **1 small cooked floury potato** and finely dice. Put the garlic and potato into a small saucepan with **1 tbsp extra virgin olive oil** and sweat lightly. Add **6 saffron threads**, ½ **tsp paprika** and ½ **tsp salt**. Pour in **200 ml/7 fl oz water** and simmer for 10 minutes. Crush the potato pieces with a fork and stir into the liquid. Leave to cool until the mixture is lukewarm, then mix with **200 ml/7 fl oz mayonnaise**.

Makes about 400 g/14 oz.

■ **Rouille sauce tastes good with cold fish or shellfish salads.**

Cocktail Sauce

Add **3 tbsp tomato ketchup, 2 tsp grated horseradish, 3 tbsp cognac** and the juice of **½ orange** to **200 ml/7 fl oz mayonnaise**. Blend with a whisk until smooth. Add a **pinch of salt, a pinch of cayenne pepper** and **3 drops Worcestershire sauce**.

Makes about 400 g/14 oz.

■ **Great as a dressing on shellfish salads.**

Dill Mustard Sauce

Finely chop **1 bunch fresh dill**. Stir in **2 tbsp coarse-grain mustard, 2 tbsp English mustard** and **5 tbsp honey** with **200 ml/7 fl oz mayonnaise**. Season to taste with **salt** and **pepper**.

Makes about 400 g/14 oz.

■ **Goes well with marinated fish salads.**

Aioli

Peel and slice **3 garlic cloves**, then grind them with **½ tsp salt** in a mortar and add to **200 ml/7 fl oz mayonnaise**. Add the juice of **½ lemon** and mix with the mayonnaise. For best results, leave to marinate for 30 minutes so the flavour of the garlic is evenly distributed and the sauce doesn't taste too hot.

Makes about 400 g/14 oz.

■ **Serve with any kind of raw vegetable or cold fish salad.**

250 g/9 oz celeriac

 1 lemon, halved

 12 walnuts

 3 apples

 ½ tsp salt

 1 tsp sugar

 pinch of pepper

 100 ml/3½ fl oz crème fraîche

 100 ml/3½ fl oz Mayonnaise
(see page 18)

Waldorf Salad

1. Peel the celeriac and rub it with a lemon half to prevent discoloration. Shell the walnuts and set them aside.

2. Peel and core the apples, removing the tops and bottoms from the fruit.

3. Grate the apple and celeriac into fine strips.

4. Put the apple and celeriac strips into a bowl. Squeeze the remaining lemon half over a sieve so the pips don't fall into the bowl. Add the salt, sugar and pepper.

5. Add the crème fraîche and the mayonnaise, mixing well.

Transfer to individual glasses, top with the walnuts, garnish with celery leaves and serve.

*
*
*
30

■ You can cut the celeriac into thin, even slices using an automatic slicer. Celeriac strips can also be blanched to achieve an even more refined flavour. Walnuts are easier to shell if you boil them briefly in equal parts milk and water.

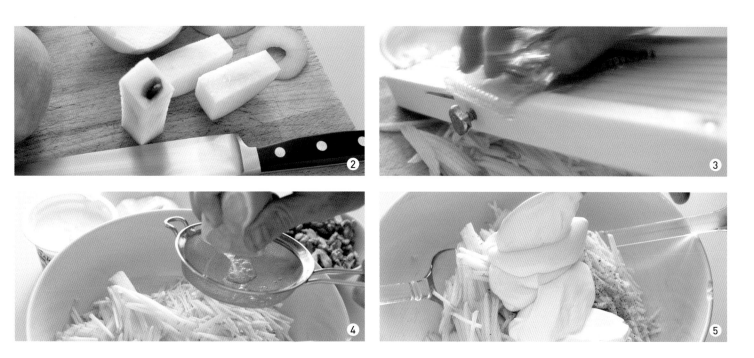

200 g/7 oz cooked pinto beans

 200 g/7 oz cooked haricot beans

 200 g/7 oz cooked broad beans

 300 g/10½ oz French beans

 salt

 3 spring onions

 pepper

 4 tbsp cider vinegar

 5 tbsp sunflower oil

 1 tbsp parsley, finely chopped

Mixed Bean Salad with Parsley

1. Put the pinto beans, haricot beans and broad beans into a bowl.

2. Cut the French beans into diagonal strips. Bring a saucepan of lightly salted water to the boil, add the French beans, bring back to the boil and cook until tender but still firm to the bite. Drain through a sieve, then refresh under cold running water.

3. Add the French beans to the pinto beans, haricot beans and broad beans.

4. Halve the spring onions and cut into thin slices. Add to the beans.

5. Add salt and pepper to taste. Pour over the vinegar and oil and mix well. Leave to marinate for 10 minutes. Add the parsley and mix.

Serve with grilled fish or veal patties.

■ You can tell if the beans are old if they break apart when soaking (left). Fresh beans stay whole (right).

2 hard-boiled eggs

 400 g/14 oz dried penne pasta

 2 spring onions

 150 g/5½ oz canned tuna in brine

 salt and pepper

 2 tbsp Mayonnaise (see page 18)

 2 tbsp natural yogurt

1 tbsp honey mustard

Pasta Salad with Tuna & Egg

1. Shell the eggs and roughly chop. Bring a large saucepan of lightly salted water to the boil, add the pasta, bring back to the boil and cook for 10 minutes, until tender but still firm to the bite. Drain, then cool under cold running water. Slice the spring onions into small rings.

2. Put the pasta, eggs and spring onions into a bowl. Drain and add the tuna.

3. Add the mayonnaise and yogurt and season to taste with salt and pepper.

4. Add the mustard and mix well.

Garnish with herbs and serve in bowls.

✳
✳
✳ **15**

■ You can make this salad with other types of pasta as well, such as farfalle, rigatoni or spaghetti.

400 g/14 oz white asparagus

 400 g/14 oz green asparagus

 2 shallots

 2 fresh mint sprigs

 ½ bunch fresh chives

 ½ bunch fresh parsley

 ½ bunch fresh chervil

 2 tbsp sugar

 2 tbsp salt

 juice of ½ lemon

 150 ml/5 fl oz Classic Vinaigrette (see page 14)

 4 eggs

 2 tbsp water

 2 tbsp cream

 1½ tbsp Mayonnaise (see page 18)

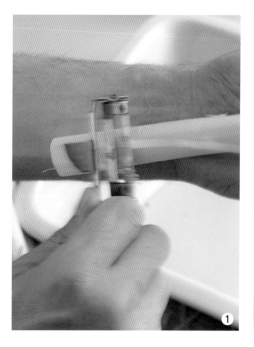

Green & White Asparagus Salad with Poached Eggs

1. Peel the white and green asparagus. Peel the shallots, cut them in half and finely chop. Cut the mint leaves into thin ribbons. Finely snip the chives. Cut the parsley and chervil leaves into ribbons.

2. Put the white asparagus, sugar, half the water, half the salt and the lemon juice into a saucepan, bring to the boil and cook for about 8 minutes. Put the green asparagus into another saucepan with the remaining water and salt, bring to the boil and and cook for about 5 minutes. Refresh the asparagus briefly in cold water. It must remain warm to absorb the marinade. Arrange the asparagus in a baking dish. Sprinkle the shallots and herbs over the asparagus stalks.

3. Pour the vinaigrette over the asparagus. Meanwhile, poach the eggs in vinegar water.

4. Gently mix the asparagus with the marinade and leave to marinate for about 10 minutes. Divide the asparagus between four plates and drizzle with the herb vinaigrette from the marinade.

Lay 1 poached egg on top of each plate of asparagus. Mix together a little of the water, cream and mayonnaise and drizzle over. Serve immediately.

■ This salad tastes great with steamed crayfish, poached quail eggs, sautéed mushrooms (such as morels), roasted veal medallions or beef steak.

✳
✳
✳ 40

 225 g/8 oz sirloin steak

 5 tbsp Thai fish sauce

200 g/7 oz cherry tomatoes

100 g/3½ oz onion

1 mango

2 tsp sugar

juice of 1½ limes

1 tbsp groundnut oil

1 tsp roasted sesame oil

5 fresh mint sprigs

1 small head of lettuce, to serve

Beef Mango Salad with Cherry Tomatoes & Mint

1. Cut the steak into strips and marinate it in 2 tablespoons of the Thai fish sauce. Cut the tomatoes into quarters. Finely dice the onion.

2. Peel and stone the mango, then cut the flesh into strips.

3. Put the onion, tomatoes, mango and sugar into a medium-sized bowl and squeeze the lime juice over.

4. Heat the groundnut oil and sesame oil in a frying pan set over a high heat. Add the steak to the pan and sear for 1 minute, turning frequently.

5. Remove the stalks from the mint leaves and set them aside as a garnish, cutting the remaining leaves into ribbons. Add the meat and the mint ribbons to the onion, tomato and mango mixture. Pour the remaining Thai fish sauce over the top and mix.

Serve in bowls on a bed of lettuce leaves, garnished with the reserved mint leaves and lime wedges.

■ Chopped, roasted peanuts or spelt berries could also lend this dish a special note.

45

8 tbsp extra virgin olive oil

 sea salt

 pepper

 5 basil leaves, cut into ribbons

 400 g/14 oz beef fillet

 juice of 1 lemon

 1 piece of Parmesan cheese

Beef Carpaccio with Parmesan Cheese & Lemon Juice

1. Use half the oil to brush four plates, then sprinkle with salt, pepper and some basil.

2. Using a long, sharp knife, cut the beef into very thin slices.

3. Lay the beef slices next to each other on the pre-seasoned plates and drizzle with the remaining oil. Add salt and pepper to taste.

4. Sprinkle with basil and drizzle over the lemon juice.

5. Grate the cheese over the beef slices using a vegetable peeler.

Serve immediately.

■ Instead of beef, you can use raw salmon, tuna or mussels, and veal fillet steak or saddle of veal.

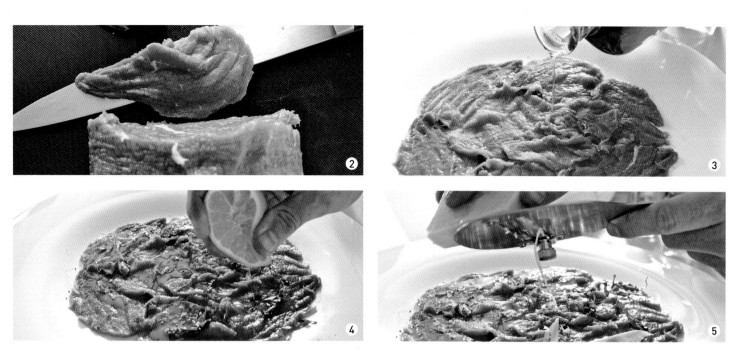

1.5 kg/3 lb 5 oz potatoes

 450 g/1 lb cucumbers

 100 g/3½ oz smoked bacon, in 1 piece

 2 onions

 200 ml/7 fl oz sunflower oil

 3 tbsp English mustard

 250 ml/9 fl oz chicken stock

 140 ml/4½ fl oz cider vinegar

 salt

 pepper

Potato & Cucumber Salad with Bacon Strips

1. Bring a large saucepan of lightly salted water to the boil, add the potatoes, bring back to the boil and cook until tender. Drain and leave to cool slightly. When cool enough to handle, peel them and cut into slices about 5 mm/¼ inch thick.

2. Peel the cucumbers and grate them into thin slices.

3. Slice the bacon, then cut into strips. Dice the onions.

4. Add the oil to a frying pan, then add the bacon and fry until crisp. Add the onions and sweat. Add the mustard and stir. Pour in the stock and vinegar and season to taste with salt and pepper. Leave to marinate for 3 minutes.

5. Pour the hot dressing over the potatoes and gently stir. Season to taste with salt and pepper.

Serve warm, garnished with sprigs of flat-leaf parsley.

* * * 50

■ Cooking the potatoes with caraway seeds will give them a spicier flavour. The salad is even tastier served with Mayonnaise (see page 18) and is a wonderful side dish for roast beef, baked fish or ham in aspic, or a variety of sausages.

2 packets dried seaweed mix

 6 tbsp soy sauce

 2 tbsp roasted sesame seeds

 2 tbsp roasted sesame oil

 300 g/10½ oz spinach leaves

1

Seaweed Salad with Spinach Leaves & Sesame Dressing

1. Soak the seaweed in lukewarm water for about 30 minutes.

2. Thoroughly drain the soaked seaweed in a colander.

3. Mix the soy sauce with the sesame seeds and the oil.

4. Rinse the spinach leaves, shake them thoroughly dry and add them to the dressing.

5. Add the drained seaweed and mix together well.

Put the salad in a bowl and serve immediately.

 **40**

■ Julienned carrots or radishes, small fried tofu squares, and small pieces of raw tuna or salmon can be mixed into the seaweed salad to give it more colour and substance. These ingredients will turn the salad into a wholesome dish.

400 g/14 oz cooked long-grain rice

 200 g/7 oz cooked ham

 200 g/7 oz canned fruit cocktail

 3 tbsp Mayonnaise (see page 18)

 1 tbsp curry powder

 salt and pepper

 juice of 1 lemon

Rice Salad with Curry Mayonnaise & Fruit

1. Put the rice and ham into a bowl.

2. Strain the fruit cocktail and cut up the large pieces if necessary.

3. Add the fruit pieces and mayonnaise to the rice.

4. Sprinkle with the curry powder, then add salt and pepper to taste and pour over the lemon juice.

5. Mix together well and leave to stand for about 30 minutes.

Serve in cocktail dishes, garnished with lettuce leaves and lemon slices.

40

■ You can use a Simple Fruit Salad (see page 60) instead of canned fruit cocktail.

Making Couscous

1. Pour **600 ml/1 pint** boiling **vegetable stock** over **250 g/9 oz couscous**. Season with **salt** and **pepper**.

2. Sprinkle over a few **saffron threads** and mix them in. Leave to soak for about 30 minutes, stirring frequently.

3. Stir in **2 tbsp olive oil** and **1 tsp butter** and serve warm as a side dish with beef or fish. Use cold for salads.

Making Bulgar Wheat

1. Bring **500 ml/18 fl oz vegetable stock** and **3 tbsp olive oil** to the boil.

2. Put **250 g/9 oz bulgar wheat** in a bowl and pour the hot stock over it.

3. Stir well and leave to soak for 1–2 hours until the bulgar wheat is as crunchy or soft as you like.

4. Use the bulgar wheat for salads, as a side dish or in fillings.

2 tomatoes

 1 white onion

 1 bunch of fresh mint, cut into ribbons, plus extra leaves to garnish

 1 tsp chopped fresh parsley

 300 g/10½ oz cooked Bulgar Wheat (see page 41)

 1 lemon

 125 ml/4 fl oz natural yogurt

 salt and pepper

 4 tbsp olive oil

Bulgar Mint Salad with Yogurt & Tomatoes

1. Dice the tomatoes and the onion.

2. Add the tomatoes, onions, mint ribbons and parsley to the bulgar wheat. Squeeze the lemon over through a sieve.

3. Add the yogurt to the salad.

4. Add salt and pepper to taste, then pour over the oil.

5. Gently combine the ingredients and leave to marinate for 30 minutes for best results.

Garnish with the reserved mint leaves and serve.

■ This recipe can also be made with couscous. Add chopped cucumber and some cooked chickpeas and season with a pinch of curry powder and some ground cumin. This variation can also be served as a side dish with Indian curries.

3 ripe tomatoes

 1 onion

 ½ garlic clove

 2 avocados

 salt and pepper

 juice of 1 lime

 3 tbsp oil

 1 tbsp vinegar

 1 bunch of fresh mint, chopped, plus extra leaves to garnish

200 g/7 oz cooked Couscous (see page 40)

onion sprouts, to garnish

Couscous Salad on Guacamole & Tomatoes

1. Finely dice the tomatoes. Peel and dice the onion. Peel and finely chop the garlic.

2. Stone the avocados and use a spoon to scoop out the flesh from the skins.

3. Season the avocado flesh with salt and pepper and drizzle the lime juice over it.

4. Using a fork, mash together until thoroughly combined.

5. Put the tomatoes, onions and garlic in a bowl and dress with the oil, vinegar, and salt and pepper to taste. Mix in the chopped mint leaves.

Put the salad on plates and top with the guacamole and couscous. Garnish with onion sprouts and mint leaves and serve immediately.

✳ ✳ ✳ 25

■ To stone the avocados, cut them in half, separate the halves from each other with a slight twist, and remove the stone.

1 small pineapple

 500 g/1 lb 2 oz cooked prawns

 300 ml/10 fl oz Cocktail Sauce (see page 21)

 orange slices, to garnish

 celery leaves, to garnish

 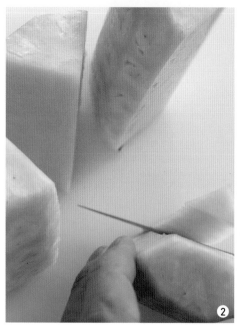

Prawn Cocktail with Cocktail Sauce

1. Remove the pineapple skin using a sharp knife.

2. Cut the pineapple into quarters lengthways and cut out the core and brown 'eyes'.

3. Cut the pineapple into 5-mm/¼-inch cubes, about the size of the prawns.

4. Place the prawns and the pineapple in a bowl, add the cocktail sauce and mix.

Serve the cocktail in small bowls, garnished with orange slices and celery leaves.

■ Wash knives and chopping boards carefully. The flavours of vegetables, onions and garlic can be passed on to fruit.

Add cooked pieces of asparagus (white and green), sautéed button mushrooms or slices of ripe peaches for another delicious version of the prawn cocktail. Decorate the cocktail dishes with finely chopped salad leaves and serve with a glass of Champagne.

500 g/1 lb 2 oz raw peeled prawns

 1 egg

 1 tbsp soy sauce

 2 tbsp unpeeled sesame seeds

 1 tbsp black sesame seeds

 1 tsp Szechuan pepper

 ½ bunch watercress

 4 tbsp Soy Vinaigrette with Coriander (see page 15)

Sautéed Sesame-coated Prawns

1. Devein the prawns. Separate the egg yolk from the white. Put the egg white and the soy sauce into a bowl and beat together.

2. Add the prawns to the mixture and marinate for about 10 minutes.

3. Mix the sesame seeds with the pepper in a bowl, add the prawns and turn.

4. Heat some sesame oil in a non-stick frying pan, add the prawns and sauté for about 2 minutes on each side. Arrange the watercress on four serving plates.

Top the watercress with the prawns, sprinkle over the soy vinaigrette and serve immediately.

■ These prawns would also be delicious on a bed of rocket, tomato or marinated asparagus salad.

1 kg/2 lb 4 oz raw octopus

 2 tbsp coarse sea salt

 1 lemon, halved, 1 half sliced

 1 sprig fresh thyme. plus extra leaves to garnish

 250 ml/9 fl oz white wine

 1 tbsp sweet paprika

 ¼ tsp cayenne pepper

 4 tbsp extra virgin olive oil

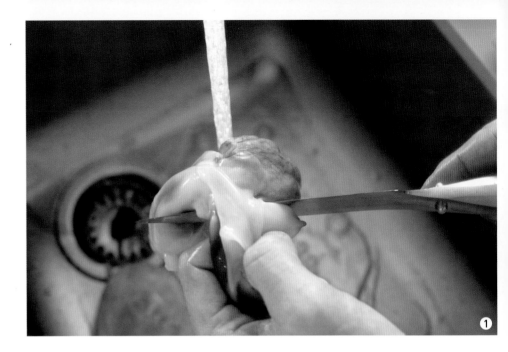

Cooked Octopus with Lukewarm Vinaigrette

1. Thoroughly wash the octopus. Turn the body inside out, pull away the entrails and cut them off with a knife.

2. Rinse thoroughly and remove any remaining skin.

3. Pinch the lower part of the head of the octopus in order to be able to grip the beak and remove it.

4. Bring a deep saucepan of lightly salted water to the boil, then add the octopus to the pan with 1 lemon slice, the thyme sprig and the white wine.

5. Bring back to the boil then simmer for about 40 minutes. Cut off a piece of the octopus and taste to check that it is cooked. To make the vinaigrette, pour the juice of half the lemon into a mixing bowl. Add the paprika and the cayenne pepper. Mix with the oil and 1 tablespoon of the hot octopus cooking liquid. Remove the octopus from the pan, drain and slice.

Arrange on plates, sprinkle some vinaigrette over and serve immediately, garnished with thyme leaves.

■ In Spain, cooked octopus is often served on cooked potato slices. It is also delicious when served with fresh garlic sauce or on a mixed bean salad. The cooking time depends largely on the size of the octopus. This is why it should be tasted to check that it is tender.

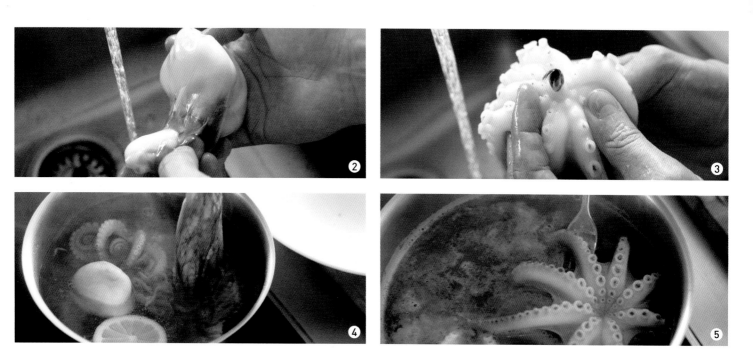

2 cooked lobsters

 1 head chicory

 200 g/7 oz mushrooms

 3½ tbsp white wine

 ½ lemon

 125 ml/4 fl oz Cocktail Sauce
(see page 21)

Lobster Cocktail with Mushrooms

1. Remove the lobster meat from the shell and cut it in half. Using the tip of a knife, pull out the vein. Reserve 1 claw per person to garnish. Cut the lobster into 5-mm/¼-inch cubes. Slice the chicory into thin ribbons, reserving 4 leaves to garnish.

2. Cut the mushrooms into quarters. Put the wine into a saucepan, bring to the boil and add the mushrooms. Squeeze the lemon over a sieve so the pips don't fall into the pan. Gently simmer for about 1 minute.

3. Drain the mushrooms in a sieve and leave to cool. Reserve the liquid to use in a fish sauce or Hollandaise sauce.

4. Put the mushrooms in a bowl with the lobster meat and cocktail sauce and mix.

Put a few chicory ribbons and 1 chicory leaf into four cocktail glasses. Fill the glasses with the cocktail and garnish with the reserved lobster claws.

■ You can make this cocktail with crabmeat or prawns and garnish with different herbs.

Types of Fruit

Unfortunately, beautiful fruit isn't always good fruit. For the most part, shrivelled organic items have more flavour than shiny fruit from the supermarket. We can seldom tell the quality of fruit from its appearance alone.

Redcurrants

Raspberries

Strawberry

Red dessert apple

Fuji apple

Golden Delicious apple

Galia melon

Cantaloupe melon

Watermelon

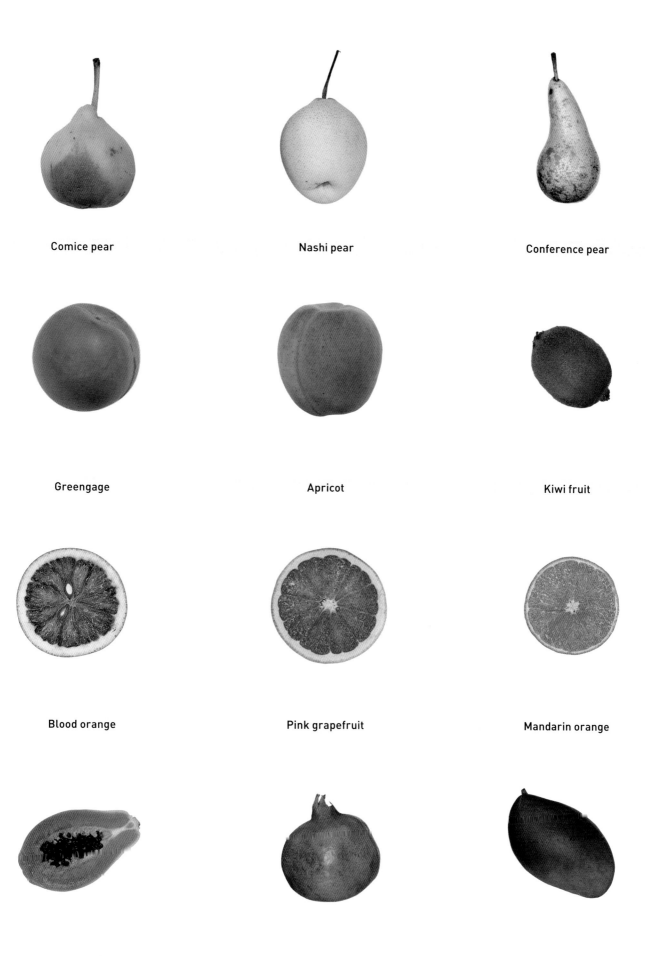

Comice pear

Nashi pear

Conference pear

Greengage

Apricot

Kiwi fruit

Blood orange

Pink grapefruit

Mandarin orange

Papaya

Pomegranate

Mango

Peeling & Stoning Mangoes

1. Remove the mango skin with a small knife or a vegetable peeler.

2. Cut off the flesh of the mango along both sides of the stone.

3. Loosen the flesh that adheres to the stone.

4. Both mango halves and the small pieces of fruit are now ready for use.

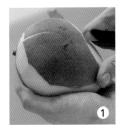

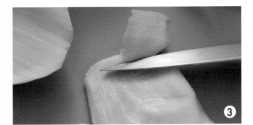

Halving & Stoning Apricots

1. Cut the apricot in half lengthways.

2. Twist the halves with your hands in opposite directions so that one half comes loose from the stone.

3. Remove the stone from the other half with a knife.

4. Use the fruit quickly as the cut surface will discolour rapidly.

Stone peaches and nectarines in the same way.

Scraping Vanilla Pods & Making Vanilla Sugar

1. Hold the vanilla pod at one end and use a sharp knife to cut the pod in half lengthways.

2. Scrape the seeds out of the whole vanilla pod with the tip of the knife.

3. Dark vanilla pods lend desserts and sauces a special aromatic taste.

4. Store the scraped-out vanilla pods with granulated sugar in a preserving jar. If the pod has hardened, put it into a food processor with the sugar and blend until you have a fine mixture.

5. In this way, you can create home-made vanilla sugar for use in the preparation of desserts, cakes and sauces.

Peeling Kiwi Fruit

1. Cut 5 mm/¼ inch off the base of the kiwi fruit and trim the top to the same extent around the core, but do not sever it completely.

2. Fold back the top and twist the top slightly to remove the little stalk.

3. Stand the kiwi fruit upright and pare the skin off.

4. Cut and use the kiwi fruit as liked.

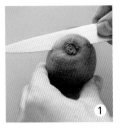
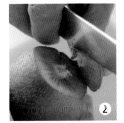

Cutting Honeydew Melons

1. Cut the melon in half lengthways.

2. Remove the seeds with a small spoon.

3. You can make little boats by dividing the melon halves several times. Remove the skin, leaving a little tag so that the flesh doesn't slip when it is being eaten.

4. Little melon balls can also be scooped out with a melon baller.

5. The scooped-out melon half can be used as a decorative bowl.

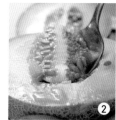

Cutting Pineapple

1. Cut a 3-cm/1¼-inch thick round off the top and the base of the pineapple.

2. Cut off the skin from top to bottom at a thickness of approximately 1 cm/ ½ inch.

3. Remove any remaining eyes with a V-shaped cut.

4. Cut the flesh into 1-cm/½-inch thick slices and scoop out the woody centre with a melon baller.

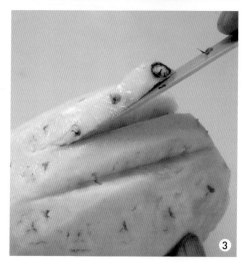

Segmenting Oranges

1. Cut a 1-cm/½-inch thick round off the top and the base of the orange.

2. Remove the outer peel and the white pith from top to bottom.

3. Holding the peeled orange in your hand, slice it into segments to the middle of the fruit, then remove the segments.

Hollowing Out Apples

1. Cut off the top 1 cm/½ inch of the apple.

2. Remove the core with a melon baller.

3. Scoop out the flesh of the apple so that it can be cooked later with a filling.

 1 honeydew melon

2 bananas

2 apples

3 oranges

250 g/9 oz red grapes

1 lime

3 tbsp honey

10 fresh mint leaves, to decorate

Simple Fruit Salad

1. Peel and halve the melon, remove the seeds with a spoon, and cut the flesh into 1 × 2-cm/½ × ¾-inch pieces. Peel the bananas and cut them into 1-cm/½-inch slices. Peel the apples, remove the core and dice the flesh into 1-cm/½-inch pieces. Slice the oranges.

2. Halve the grapes and remove the seeds with the tip of the knife.

3. Squeeze the lime through a sieve over the fruit salad, so that none of the pulp is included. The acid will prevent the fruit discolouring. Add the honey and the chopped mint and mix.

Chill the fruit salad and serve, garnished with the mint leaves.

 20

■ Make sure that you toss the salad very well in the lime juice, otherwise the bananas and apples will discolour very quickly. If you are going to chill the salad for more than 1 hour, do not add the bananas until just before serving.

½ honeydew melon

1 mango

3 oranges

3 kiwi fruit

2 limes

60 g/2¼ oz Vanilla Sugar
(see page 57)

4 passion fruit

6 strawberries

pinch of lime zest, to decorate

1 vanilla pod, to decorate

2 tbsp grated coconut, to decorate

Exotic Fruit Salad

1. Remove the melon seeds with a spoon, and scoop out balls of flesh with a melon baller. Peel the mango and cut it in half, remove the stone and dice the flesh. Peel and segment the oranges. Peel the kiwi fruit, cut in half and slice.

2. Wash the limes in hot water. Squeeze them by hand and add them to the salad. The active oils in the zest will add an even more exotic taste to the fruit salad.

3. Add the sugar. Cut the passion fruit in half, scoop out the insides with a spoon and add to the salad. Leave to marinate for 30 minutes. Remove the limes from the salad. Thinly slice the strawberries lengthways and use to decorate the salad.

Decorate with the lime zest, vanilla pod and grated coconut. Arrange the salad in the hollowed-out melon half and serve.

■ To keep the remaining melon half fresh for longer, do not remove the seeds, tightly wrap the melon half in clingfilm and store on a lower shelf of the refrigerator. It will keep for up to 3 days.

INDEX